THE INEVITABILITY OF WRITING

A Case Study About Theresa

Oluwasolami Ajayi

ISBN-20: 9798686877047
ISBN-10: 1477123456

Cover design by: Art Painter
Library of Congress Control Number: 2018675309
Printed in the United States of America

CONTENTS

ACKNOWLEDGEMENT

This book would not have been possible without the help of Mr. Solomon Okpa who has helped organize this manuscript. Special thanks to my parents Mr and Mrs Ajayi, my brother Fikayo for their encouragement and support always.

To my teachers and to everyone who have in one way or the other contributed to the success of this book; God bless you all.

FOREWORD

"Writing is a major tool for self- instruction and self-development."

INTRODUCTION

This is a concise book that is written to let you know the practical importance of applying writing into your everyday life. Are you finding it hard to express your mind? Can you express your mind but can't seem to find someone to listen to you? Do your words get hanged in the air while trying to voice out your opinions? Are you overwhelmed by your emotions already? You can become a survivor. I implore you to give this book a chance. Find out how you can become a survivor by taking a short walk with me through this book.

CHAPTER ONE

THE CONCEPT OF WRITING

WHAT IS WRITING?

Writing is a form of communication that allows us to put our feelings and ideas on paper. It enables us to input our knowledge and belief into convincing arguments by conveying meaning through a well-constructed text.

Writing may be defined as any conventional system of marks or signs that represents the utterances of a language. It renders language visible and long lasting whereas speech is ephemeral.

According to Wikipedia, writing is a medium of human communication that involves the representation of a language with words, symbols and lots more. It relies on many of the semantic structures as the speech it represents with the added dependency of a system of symbols to represent that language's phonology and morphology. The result of this activity is called a *Text*. The interpreter or the activator of this text is called a *Reader*.

CHAPTER TWO

APPRAISALS OF WRITING

Writing has been appraised in different ways by various people. I will be listing few of them below:

'Writing is a socially acceptable form of Schizophrenia'[E.L. Doctorow]

'Writing is a struggle against silence'[Carles Fuentes]

'Writing is the only way to talk without being interrupted'[Julius Renard]

'Writing makes no noise except groans which is done alone'[Ursula K. Lenguin

'Writing is concrete and permanent'

WRITING AS A SOCIALLY ACCEPTABLE FORM OF SCHIZOPHRENIA

"She wasn't thinking clearly, everything before her was a blur. She wondered what she has done to deserve her kind of life. She is like a virus everyone avoids wherever she goes. Even her parents had started to avoid her since they discovered she has Schizophrenia. Of course no one wants to get associated with a mentally disturbed person. She took out her diary and let out her feelings as tears flow freely down her face. She felt relieved once again as she shared her emotions with the only thing that never avoids her".

Schizophrenia is a mental disorder that affect a person's ability to think, feel and behave clearly. In the short context above, even though Theresa has just been diagnosed of Schizophrenia, it didn't stop her from writing. Even though her life was a blur, she kept on writing and even though she wasn't thinking clearly, she still poured out her mind. Aren't you wondering what the reason is? It is because writing has been socially accepted as a form of Schizophrenia. That means some people have gotten so used to writing that they can write in any frame of mind they find themselves. You see how I wrote 'some people'. It doesn't apply to everyone, most people write only when they are in the mood.

WRITING AS A STRUGGLE AGAINST SILENCE

She struggled to remain silent as her bullies pushed her to the ground.   She was abused verbally. They called her all kinds of name because she was different from them. Her instinct urged her to give them back as they are doing to her but what good will that bring? They will continue hurting her if she tried opening her mouth to talk, so she decided to ignore them like she has always done. They left her to take care of her bruises alone when they got tired of bullying her as usual. She managed to walk back home before shedding any tears. She had no friends to share her problems with. She couldn't even tell her parents about what she was facing in school. They were already so stressed up when they discovered she was mentally ill. So she shared her pains with the only one thing that has always had her back; HER DIARY.

According to Carles Fuentes, writing can serve as a struggle against silence. There are situations whereby you aren't supposed to keep quiet. You ought to voice out your opinions yet you have no choice than to compromise your silence because of the situation you find yourself. In the end, the only option you have is to write out your pains like Theresa did. Even though Theresa couldn't speak back to her bullies, she was able to write everything inside her most prized possession.

WRITING IS THE ONLY WAY TO TALK WITHOUT BEING INTERRUPTED

She was insulted and humiliated before the whole class. She wanted to stand up for herself but she was asked to keep quiet. Her whole class defamed her before the teacher and she believed them. Why wouldn't she? She was the only one standing against the whole class, even the whole school. However, she made a decision to vindicate herself. She decided to stand up against the whole school but she is faced with a problem. She finds it difficult to freely express herself, so her decision was rendered useless. She picked up her pen and book, pouring out her feelings, emotions and deepest pain. They came out in a tide of waves, relieving her of all her pent-up emotions. She was free to express her mind once again without any interruption.

Here, we see that Theresa couldn't freely express her mind probably because that's just her nature. Even when she tried, she was interrupted. It brings us to the fact that we can always be interrupted during our speech. Writing on the other hand is free of any interruption. You are free to write as much as you want without disturbance from anyone.

WRITING AS GROANS WHICH MAKE NO NOISE

"She has been doing this for the past thirteen years. Dealing with her infirmities quietly, making silent groans which cannot be uttered. Sitting down alone on the cold floor in the corner of her room, she confided in her diary yet again."

According to Franz Kafia; '*Writing is utter solitude, the descent into the abyss of yourself'.* This means you can write in utter solitude completing forgetting everyone and everything around you. It's like when you are so engrossed in writing immeasurably to the extent that you are completely oblivious of your time and surroundings.

From the context above, we discover that Theresa has been abused both physically and emotionally. She couldn't find it in herself to deal with her problems. Rather, she makes a noiseless groan daily while writing in her diary. We read how she deals with her problem alone by writing out her emotions in form of groans. Therefore, writing makes no noise, it only makes silent groans which cannot be spoken.

WRITING IS CONCRETE AND PERMANENT

The greatest edge that writing has over speaking is that it is concrete and long-lasting. There is a saying that '*the faintest pen is sharper than the sharpest brain'.* There is a limit to what the human brain can take, even the sharpest brain can't take everything in. On the other hand, if you put anything into writing, you'd meet them in the same way you put them after many years. Any contract between two or more persons cannot be binding until they sign a legal document which is also engraved in a **Book**. This brings us back to the fact that writing is subjected to permanence. Can you see that writing cannot be avoided?

CHAPTER THREE

WHY WRITING IS INEVITABLE

What does INEVITABLE mean?

The word INEVITABLE means 'impossible to avoid' or 'impossible to prevent'. The synonyms are inescapable and unavoidable.

What does WRITING IS INEVITABLE means?

Since Inevitable means 'Unavoidable', then it means writing is unavoidable. Writing is something that cannot be avoided, no one can escape holding a pen to write. Even little kids learn how to write in nursery class, writing is something that is being taught to every literate person right from their childhood. However, there are some people who possess the special gift of writing. They are the ones who has the craving to share their ideas and perspective with others. They'd go to any extent to make sure their dream of becoming a writer is fulfilled. We have so many great writers today who has made good use of their writing skills. Writers like Joyce Meyers, Esther Odukoya and so many others made great use of their talents by inspiring others through their books. Had it been that they didn't value their writing talent, they won't be able to inspire us today. *'If you don't treat your talent with value, then it won't value you either'*. Start writing now!

REASONS WHY PEOPLE WRITE

People write for different reasons. Their differences make them unique. Here are the reasons:

1. The primary reason for writing anything is to communicate with others by stimulating interest in their readers.

2. Writing is used to reflect on your experiences and learn from

them.

3. People write for themselves.

4. People write for others.

5. People write in order to see their thoughts clearly.

6. People write to view their perspectives as it changes regularly.

7. Writing can serve as a fun pass time

8. You can write your thoughts to make an impact

9. People use writing to voice out their concern

10. People write for their passion

I will explain few of these reasons below:

-WRITING AS A REFLECTION ON EXPERIENCE

"Now Theresa has achieved a lot. She is all grown up as an independent woman, all traces of the past now eradicated. She decided to share her story with the world. She wanted to let them know that the 'The Once Rejected Stone has become the 'Chief Cornerstone'. No one seem to recognize her as the once rejected social outcast. She brought out her old diary. She re-drafted it, going through the many process of writing. Then she had it published. Her book went viral. People were shocked to read the successful story of the old social outcast. Theresa was able to show everyone that they didn't break her. Yes! She was humiliated for 18 years of her life but she wasn't broken. She is stronger than they will ever be"

Theresa, publishing her diary out to the public isn't meant to condemn any of her bullies but to reflect on her bitter experiences. I'm sure that when people get to see her story, they'd be greatly inspired. People that are still in her shoes will get to learn from her experience. The greatest thing is that the bullies might get to have a change of heart. Can you imagine what would have happened if Theresa had not been writing down her bitter experiences? How will she inspire people? How will she publish her diary if she hadn't written them down? Even if she tried writing about her past when she is all grown up, it will be so hard to start racking her brain about her past.

Therefore, writing helps to reflect on experiences, thereby stimulating interest or action from the reader.

-WRITING FOR OURSELVES

When we write for ourselves, it helps us to think, learn and understand. Writing for ourselves is the same thing as writing about ourselves. It is a private affair although it can be shared with others like Theresa did. I'm sure it had never crossed Theresa's mind to share her diary with the public while she was still the 'well known social outcast' but she felt the need to do that as soon as she became a self-fulfilled person. She wrote for herself but ended up sharing with others.

-WRITING FOR OTHERS

Writing for others is the sole job of a writer or author. They make story out of anything and share with the general public. When we write for others, it is usually for assessment or publication for a wider readership. I have learnt a lot from various authors who write for 'others' like me. You can also learn from others.

-PEOPLE WRITE IN ORDER TO SEE THEIR THOUGHTS CLEARLY

Most of the time, the thoughts, feelings, emotions, insecurities, even problems are buried deep in our heart. It's at the tip of our tongues at times and yet, we can't share it. Writing helps to see the clarity in our thinking. You can innovate different ideas, destroy the negative ones, find solution to the presiding ones and generate new ones after writing out your thoughts.

After so many years, Theresa was able to re-organize her thought and feelings which was engraved in her diary. She was able to see through her state of mind, her thoughts, condition and the most important thing is that she found a solution to it.

-PEOPLE WRITE TO VIEW THEIR RATIONAL PERSPECTIVES

Your ideas, perspectives and vision will not remain the same forever. They tend to change a lot as the world does because that's how growth happens. Having a written record on our perspectives helps us to reflect on how far we have come. After so many years of pain and torture, Theresa was able to see how far she has come. She saw her life in a new dimension, definitely her perspective about life changed. She made use of her written record to inspire the world.

WRITING TO VOICE OUT CONCERN

Is any social cause close to your heart? Do you want to make some positive impact in the society? Then voice out your concern through writing. Do the volunteer job! Probably your community is facing some challenges and no one is able to stand up for the community, you can do it by writing, thereby sharing your concerns with the concerned person or persons.

WRITING TO MAKE AN IMPACT

The words you write can inspire, guide and bring out a change in people. Writing out your thoughts or experience can go a long way. Theresa was able to make an impact by sharing her experiences with people.

WRITING AS A FUN PASS TIME

Whenever I'm bored, I jot down random titles and start writing on them. I tend to make story out of anything. It's a great exercise to do while passing time. It is fun!

-WRITING FOR THE ZEAL AND PASSION

These set of people are the ones with the talent of writing of writing, they are committed to getting the job done because of their zeal and drive to write. These people are always ready to make their visions get realized. I love writing right from childhood. Even though I tend to write nonsense then, I have started to make sense out of my nonsense now.

CHAPTER FOUR

THE POSITIVE IMPACTS OF WRITING

Here are the positive impacts of writing:

1. Writing is fixed, therefore more concrete and permanent. Like I said in chapter two that there is a limit to what the sharpest brain can take, I am saying the same here again. You can't store up everything in your brain, you have to document the important things for future use. Even the brain gets tired but the book cannot. Can you see how important it is to WRITE.

2. The process of writing is something that you can constantly learn from. Getting cumulative feedback and reflecting on your writing can help you develop. However, an important benefit of writing is that it serves as a form of assessment. A piece can be self-contained with its own package and a particular purpose. Therefore, writing helps people to continually examine and re-assess themselves.

3. Writing sometimes has more impact than other communication channels. Through writing, you can select a language to influence the thoughts and actions of your reader in particular ways, guiding them through your evidence and argument to convince them of your book analysis and conclusions. Theresa was able to inspire people with the story of her life because she has an evidence to convince them that her book is indeed real. Her evidence are the writings in her old diary.

4. Writing enables reviews and previews: Have it in mind

that you do not have to submit your first draft. Your first draft can be filled with all kinds of error and that's why you have the opportunity to review before submission. You can change your write-up as much as you can until you get the desired result. You can keep coming back to a previous piece of writing so as to gain more benefit from reviewing it as a result. Looking back at your previous experiences can help you learn more about your writing style. How do you intend to look back into your past work if you haven't been writing them down? Can you see for a fact that you have to write?

5. Writing Offers You Time And Space to Re-draft and Re-focus Your Book: In this way, writing is easier than spoken communication. While speaking, you might not even think before voicing out how you feel or what you want. Even when you think of words, you have to immediately release them to the audience and once it is spoken, there is no opportunity to edit them before they are heard. On the other hand, writing offers you the opportunity to re-draft your message until you are satisfied with it. You can edit your book before they are sent out to your audience. Theresa could have said anything in exasperation when she was bullied but she didn't. She knew she won't be able to take her words back once it is heard. Therefore, she always waits till whenever she is in her right mind before pouring out her feelings into her diary.

6. It Helps You Think Through Problems: Writing helps us to analyse our thoughts and think through our problems. How could Theresa have dealt with her problems if she hadn't confided in her diary? Whenever I feel stuck or I'm contemplating a problem, it helps to write them down and work through possible solutions to them.

7. Written Words Influences The Society: In our contemporary world, journalist, bloggers, speechwriters and the clique can't do anything without these written

words. How we think as a society is largely thanks to what people write. Writing has changed the world in ways we least expect. Even Theresa was able to inspire the society with her written works.

8. *No History Without Writing: We wouldn't have our history if there are no writers. There is a popular saying that 'History is written by the victors'. If we don't write them down, we would not have them all. Another history goes that 'History has a way of repeating itself". How will we know the history if it isn't documented. We have the great historic book which is the Bible. The gospel of Jesus wouldn't travel as far and as wide as it is today if the Blibical Authors hadn't written it.*

9. *Everyone Has A Book Inside Them: I think everyone has a book inside them whether they like it or not.. It's not necessarily a book of fiction, it could be a book of experience like Theresa's. I've had books inside me all my life even though I started with a sucky writing. You have to develop that book inside you. The only way you can achieve that is by practicing how to write. Why do you think autobiographies are popular? People want to share their stories because they have a story to tell. Writing is the only way to get that story into the hands of people that care.*

10. *You Are More Likely To Achieve Written Goals: Depending on your personality, telling people about your goals can either help or hurt you. When you tell people your goals beforehand, you may end up not achieving them. Writing them down for everyone might be an important step in actually achieving your goals. According to research from the Dominican University in California, 'You are 42 percent more likely to achieve your goals if you write them down". Will you take this odd today?*

CHAPTER FIVE

What are you focused on today? Are you ready to get started? Are you still finding it difficult to express your mind to people? Can you express your mind but can't find someone to listen to you? Do you struggle with your deepest fears and insecurities and can't tell them to anyone? Do words get hanged up in your mind while trying to voice out your opinions? Have you become overwhelmed with your thoughts and emotions? Then you must have seen Theresa's story. She was only able to rise above her problems because of WRITING.

Coming this far with me, you must have learnt the importance of writing through Theresa's story. Theresa was an 18 years old girl who suffered schizophrenia because of the way life dealt with her. She has been referred to as 'the social outcast' since she was five. She was left alone by everyone. Theresa doesn't have a friend, yet she managed to share her deepest fears and emotions with her diary. However, two things were needful for her, God and her diary. God never left her side neither did she forget God through it all. She didn't let go of her diary either.

Writing is hard work, not magic. It begins with deciding why you are writing and whom you are writing for. What are your intentions? Writing is about making a serious time commitment and getting the work done. For you to write, you need to take up life lessons which will help you level up. More social events, activity and research must be done. Your knowledge will increase as you try to write more.

Jesus said, 'I am the Alpha and the Omega, the Beginning and the End, the First and the Last'. If you live by this words, x-ray your motives and yield it all to God, then you come to an end and you can zip it up.

You can face whatever is ahead of you and with Christ as your strength, you can succeed. It is my prayer that this book should be an answer to one of your prayer points.